Debra Oswald is a writer for stage, film, television and children's fiction.

Her stage plays have been produced around Australia. *Gary's House*, *Sweet Road* and *The Peach Season* were all shortlisted for the NSW Premier's Award. Her play *Dags* has had many Australian productions and has been published and performed in Britain and the United States. *Gary's House* has been on the senior high school syllabus, and has been performed in translation in both Denmark and Japan. *The Peach Season* won the 2005 Seaborn Playwright's Prize. *Mr Bailey's Minder* broke the Griffin Theatre's box office record in 2004, toured nationally in 2006, and was produced in Philadelphia in 2008.

Debra has written two plays for the Australian Theatre for Young People. *Skate* was performed in Sydney, on a NSW country tour and at the Belfast Theatre Festival. *Stories in the Dark* premiered at Riverside Theatre Parramatta in 2007.

She is the author of three 'Aussie Bite' books for kids, including *Nathan and the Ice Rockets*, and five novels for teenage readers: *Me and Barry Terrific*, *The Return of the Baked Bean*, *The Fifth Quest*, *The Redback Leftovers* and *Getting Air*.

Among Debra's television credits are 'Bananas in Pyjamas', 'Sweet and Sour', 'Palace of Dreams', 'The Secret Life of Us' and award-winning episodes of 'Police Rescue'.

Clare Testoni as the Miller's Wife and Robert Braine as the Miller in the 2007 atyp production. (Photo: Allan Vella)

STORIES IN THE DARK

DEBRA OSWALD

Currency Press, Sydney

CURRENCY TEENAGE SERIES

First published in 2008
by Currency Press Pty Ltd,
PO Box 2287, Strawberry Hills, NSW, 2012, Australia.
enquiries@currency.com.au
www.currency.com.au

NATIONAL LIBRARY OF AUSTRALIA CIP DATA

Author:	Oswald, Debra.
Title:	Stories in the dark / author, Debra Oswald
Publisher:	Strawberry Hills, N.S.W.: Currency Press, 2008.
ISBN:	9780868198316 (pbk.)
Dewey Number:	A822.3

Typeset for Currency Press by Dean Nottle.
Cover design by Laura McLean, Currency Press.
Front cover image © atyp
Back cover shows Tyrone Lindqvist as Neighbour 1, Caroline Main as Anna,
Claudia Tory as Hunter's Wife, Barton Ware as Hunter and Noni Hollonds as
Neighbour 2 in the 2007 atyp production. (*Photo: Allan Vella*)

Contents

Currency Press acknowledges the Traditional Owners of the Country on which we live and work. We pay our respects to all Aboriginal and Torres Strait Islander Elders, past and present.

Director's Note

Towards the end of *Stories in the Dark*, a 12-year-old boy, Tomas, tries to explain why he likes stories and folktales. He struggles to articulate a reason for something he knows is deeply important to him, something that is of enormous personal value and yet, at the same time, difficult to grasp.

This is the core of Debra Oswald's play. *Stories in the Dark* is a kind of dramatic tug-of-war centring on the worth of stories in a time of extreme crisis. During the rehearsal period for our production the cast and crew actively wrestled with this issue throughout the process. At times we felt we agreed with Anna, the 16-year-old, that stories are 'childish rubbish'. At other times we felt that the simple joy of a tale well told was a great gift for our terrified characters.

In the end we disagreed with Anna. (Perhaps not surprisingly, as good theatre is, after all, good storytelling.) Wisdom from the past never intends to solve present problems. This is a promise stories never make. However they do function to remind us of our humanity, to imagine a world other than our own where a theme, event or action may impact on our own dilemmas. Stories ask us to listen to their wisdom and make of it what we will. Like in the theatre, those who receive the story have a role to play; they must interpret the story and, potentially, discover something meaningful that does change their present.

And there is something else; where the simple act of telling a mysterious, surprising, funny and fantastical tale is, perhaps most importantly, reason enough.

Stories in the Dark presents wonderful challenges for any theatre group or school tackling the play. Debra's play is constructed around the telling of six complete stories. These tales call for ogres, giants, blind kings, wolves and many other creatures of fantasy all to be fully realised on stage. So when I first read the play, it was, well, a little daunting! But this is what is great about it. The play can be performed by a cast of 60 or ten. It can be performed using a wild array of costumes and prosthetics or, if you choose, with nothing but the actors' craft and a few cardboard boxes. As you will see from the photos in this volume, atyp used masks as the central performance aesthetic for the telling of our stories. This helped with the speed of the overall production and helped with the quick changes. But this is only one solution among many: each production will be different. The play is a great challenge where the whole cast and crew can come together to work out how to tell the stories in the best way.

Timothy Jones

Timothy Jones Artistic Director of atyp and directed the first production of *Stories in the Dark* in 2007.

Playwright's Note

Sometimes I get the spark for writing a new play when I suddenly find a connection between two of my obsessions. That's how *Stories in the Dark* came about.

When I was a kid, I was fascinated by folk stories and borrowed armloads of library books of myths and tales. In recent years, I discovered the great store of tales on the internet. I would lose myself on the net for hours, following trails of story from one website to another. I found myself back at the local library, trawling for books of legends again. But I had no idea how I would ever use this fascination with folk tales in my own work.

Around the same time, I became interested in the struggle of the international legal system to find justice for victims of war and genocide. I was reading books about Rwanda and the former Yugoslavia but I didn't imagine such reading would find its way into my own work. And I had no idea those two interests of mine would intersect.

During rehearsals for another play, I got chatting to one of the actors: the wonderful Maggie Blinco. We shared our love of folk tales and Maggie told me a delightful story about performing in the musical *Oliver*. At the beginning of the second act, Maggie and the young actor playing the lead role would sit on a piece of scenery suspended high above the stage. They had to wait there in darkness for twenty minutes until their cue to be lowered onto the stage. To pass the time, Maggie would tell the boy a story, whispering it aloud. Eventually, Maggie ran out of stories. She began reading from books of traditional tales by the light of day so she would have a fresh story to relay to the young actor each night in the dark, high above the stage.

I loved Maggie's story and it helped me click an idea into place. I would throw the world of folk tales into the middle of a dark place—a contemporary, painful situation where the stakes are very high for two kids trapped in a war-torn city. For Anna and Tom's story, I've drawn details from the siege of Sarajevo but the setting could be many times and places.

Folk tales, from many different cultures, are an extraordinarily rich form. I love the way they offer exotica and earthiness, slapstick comedy and heartbreaking moments, disturbing ideas and nourishing ideas, connecting us to the wisdom of previous generations, feeding our yearning to imagine a world where things are fair, lucky, potentially magical.

Stories are a way to imagine ourselves through dilemmas and emotional blows we might have to face one day, so they can be part of our moral and spiritual education. During a time of crisis and dislocation, the tales can remind us that other kinds of life went on before this and will happen after this.

There's something about the simplicity and mystery of folk tales told aloud that can draw listeners in, sneaking around our opinionatedness and prejudices, to touch us deeply. Many of the stories are surprisingly dark, fatalistic and funny, facing the reality of death and suffering, urging us to endure and try to laugh at life's grim elements.

Then again, should we regard most folk and fairytales as just romanticised, escapist fantasies? Do they anaesthetise us and trick people into expecting the world to be fair when it's not? Are such stories inadequate, absurd or even offensive in the face of ugly reality? Or can they help the human spirit to survive? These are some of the questions I wanted to explore in *Stories in the Dark*.

I had a great long list of tales I wanted to draw from but only a few would fit into this one play. The first story, 'The Ogre's Three Golden Hairs', is a pretty straight adaptation of the Grimm brothers' version. But the Grimm brothers were themselves retelling a traditional tale which exists in other versions. Many of its story elements—the abandoned baby rescued by a childless couple, a boy sent on an impossible quest, etc.—pop up in countless tales.

One of the fascinating things when you read tales from different cultures is the way strikingly similar elements crop up in stories from all over the world. A good example is the image of 'singing bones'—the idea of the bones of a murdered person crying out for truth and justice. There are singing bones stories from Africa, Scotland, India, Russia and elsewhere.

With the tales for the play, I felt free to scrounge chunks from various traditional stories and glue them together, adding my own variations, settings and twists. For a story like 'The Ice Dragon and the She-wolf', I fished bits from the sea of folk tales—a village terrorised by a dragon, a woman trapped in an enchanted animal skin, a mother's sacrifice, an extreme landscape, the power of true love, etc.—and I used them in my own combination to create a 'new' story which would do what I needed for that moment in the play. That's exactly how folk stories work, constantly adapting and borrowing.

In choosing stories, the most important goal was to create a powerful chemistry between the tales Anna and Tom tell each other at night and the daytime story of their struggles in the city. In the end, I wanted this play to be about the power of stories and the limits of stories, about friendship, loss and survival.

The cast and creative team of the atyp production then faced the job of handling this odd mixture—creating the grim, dangerous reality of a city in war as well as bringing fantastical folk tales to life on stage. We had a lot of fun creating ogres, princes, she-wolves, toxic dragon poo, singing bones and the rest.

I want to thank the Literature Board of the Australia Council, Richard Glover, Maggie Blinco and Michael Wynne, everyone at atyp and Riverside Theatres. I'm grateful to the fabulous creative team and young cast of the atyp production whose ideas helped shape this play. Most importantly, I have to thank Timothy Jones who supported and guided the project from its beginning as a two-sentence notion right through to doing a great job of directing the first production.

Debra Oswald

Australian Government

Australia Council
for the Arts

The author received assistance for this project from the Australian Government through the Australia Council, its arts funding and advisory body.

Claudia Tory as the Ogre's Grandmother and Tyrone Lindqvist as the Boy in the 2007 atyp production. (Photo: Allan Vella)

First Production

Stories in the Dark was first produced by australian theatre for young people (atyp) and Riverside Theatres at the Lennox Theatre, Riverside Theatres Parramatta, on 30 April 2007, with the following cast:

Tomas	Cooper Torrens
Anna	Caroline Main
Miller, Ferryman, Elf, Farmer Jones, Villager, Child Puppeteer, Nick	Robert Braine
Miller's Wife, Townsperson, Woman 2, Musician 2, Lazy Gus, Woman in Coat, She-wolf/Katerina	Clare Testoni
Boy, Man in Jacket, Serge, Fisherman, Villager, Neighbour 1, Potato-head Boy	Tyrone Lindqvist
Princess, Woodcutter's Wife, Blackmarket Woman, Lazy Gus's Wife, Woman in Water Queue, Anoushka, Neighbour 2	Noni Hollonds
Nasty King, Station Guard, Doctor, Horse, Ivan	Kyle Hedrick
Townsperson, Man 1, Woodcutter, Peter, Villager, Hunter	Barton Ware
Ogre's Grandmother, Woman Neighbour, Musician 1, Mrs Brown, Woman 3, Villager, Hunter's Wife	Claudia Tory
Ogre, Sardine Man, Blind King, Cheerful Man, Villager, Man in Water Queue	Dean Mason

Director, Timothy Jones
Assistant Director, Danielle O'Keefe
Set and Costume Designer, Jo Briscoe
Lighting Designer, Sydney Bouhaniche
Composer and Sound Designer, Max Lambert

Characters

Anna
Tomas

All the other roles can be performed by an ensemble of six or more actors:

Miller	**Doctor**
Miller's Wife	**King**
Boy	**Serge**
Nasty King	**Peter**
Princess	**Musician 1**
Ferryman	**Musician 2**
Ogre's Grandmother	**Blackmarket Woman**
Ogre	**Woman in Coat**
Man in Jacket	**Villagers**
Sardine Man	**Dragon**
Cheerful Man	**Ivan**
Gus's Wife	**Katerina/She-wolf**
Lazy Gus	**Anoushka**
Mrs Brown	**Hunter**
Fisherman	**Hunter's Wife**
Farmer Jones	**Neighbour 1**
Horse	**Neighbour 2**
Woman Neighbour	**Nick**
Station Guard	**Potato-Head Boy**

Various men and women in queues, city streets, townspeople, party guests

Setting

City streets and a derelict house in a war-torn city, such as Sarajevo.

ACT ONE

Scene One

Night. A once-grand city house, battered by mortar shells. There are a few bits of furniture half buried under rubble.

A sixteen-year-old girl, ANNA, enters and switches on the unbroken bulbs on the ornate light fitting. She drags in a car battery and fetches plastic bags which she dumps onto the floor.

A boy lurches up from behind a pile of junk—TOMAS. He's disoriented, terrified, but full of bravado. His sudden appearance makes ANNA yell out with fright, ready to defend herself.

Anna What are you doing? Get out!

> *When she sees it's just a kid, she relaxes a little.*

You shouldn't skulk around like that!

> *TOMAS grabs a hunk of wood as a weapon.*

Tomas Don't come near me!

Anna Whoa… I'm not going anywhere near you.

> *TOMAS lowers the weapon.*

Tomas Who are you? Was I asleep? Must've fallen asleep.

Anna Yeah, well, whatever. Get out.

Tomas Is this your house?

Anna No.

Tomas You can't tell me to get out if it's not your house.

Anna Yeah? Is that what you reckon, you little insect?

> *She grabs a broken chair.*

Get out now or I'll wrap this round your stupid head.

> *TOMAS gets ready to defend himself with the hunk of wood.*

Tomas I'll fight you.

> *ANNA snorts a laugh and drops the chair.*

Anna Oh, I'm too tired. Go back to where you came from.

TOMAS doesn't answer. ANNA scrutinises him.

Ah, you're a country bumpkin, I bet. A farm boy.

TOMAS shrugs.

You and your family dig potatoes and push goats around?

Tomas Well, on our farm, we've got— [pigs and fruit trees]

Anna Yeah, whatever. You're in the city now, potato-brain. And the point is, this is my spot, so you can't stay here.

Tomas I don't want to stay here anyway.

Anna Excellent. You'd better get going.

Tomas [*peering out the window*] Is it night already?

Anna Hey, bring any food with you from the farm? A cabbage? A few carrots?

TOMAS shakes his head. ANNA casts a disdainful eye over him—that'd be right.

She rummages through the plastic bags to find various items.

She untangles a string of party lights and hooks them up to the car battery.

Tomas What's that for?

Anna Word is the power's getting cut off tonight. I'm going to be ready.

Tomas That's dumb. They're not even proper lights.

Anna These little guys suck up less power. So the battery'll last longer.

Tomas But they'll fix the electricity.

Anna You understand nothing, cabbage-head. In this city, we've been putting up with crap for months now. A thousand different kinds of crap. And I bet we don't even rate thirty seconds on the world news anymore. I bet—

ANNA realises she's gone into a rave and confused TOMAS.

Look, the militia—the arseholes over there shooting at us—they cut off the power and water when it suits them.

Tomas You stole that car battery and the party lights.

Anna [*laughing*] Do you think anyone's planning a party tonight?

2

A mortar exploding in a neighbouring street makes TOMAS jump with fright.

Oh, must be the party fireworks.

Tomas That was a shell. A mortar.

Anna The kid's a genius.

TOMAS peers anxiously out the window.

How old are you?

Tomas Almost thirteen.

Anna Twelve.

Tomas How old are you?

Anna A hundred and five.

Tomas I'm not stupid. You can't talk to me like I'm stupid.

TOMAS goes to leave.

Anna Really? Where are you off to now?

Tomas Wherever you're supposed to go until they find your parents.

Anna Listen, carrot-boy, don't go out unless you know exactly where you're going.

Tomas I'm not a carrot-boy. I have a name—Tomas. And I'm going.

Anna There's a curfew for a reason. In the day, there are snipers, stray mortars, but at night, it's way uglier. At night, either side could shoot you.

Tomas I can look after myself.

TOMAS has been selecting the best weapon for himself from the piles of rubble.

ANNA watches him, then laughs.

Anna Boys. Stupid boys. You won't keep that head on your shoulders for very long.

Another explosion outside makes TOMAS tremble.

Tomas Soldiers bashed in our door in the middle of the night, shouting, said we had ten minutes to pack our stuff.

Anna I bet, in the end, they only gave you two minutes.

Tomas They made everyone get on trucks but we all ended up on different ones. When the truck stopped in another town, I snuck out, tried to find someone from my family but it was too dark.

3

Anna So what—did the soldiers catch you?

Tomas No. I hid in a ditch until it got light.

Anna Your parents are in the city now?

Tomas I think so but I don't—I'll find the place you're supposed to go to get everything sorted out. But probably night time isn't the best time.

Anna No, it isn't, you cabbage-headed moron.

> *TOMAS is fighting tears. ANNA sighs, annoyed.*

You can sleep over there tonight. Do whatever in the morning.

> *ANNA drags out her bedding, carefully rolled and hidden behind rubble.*
>
> *TOMAS looks through debris to find something to sleep on.*

Tomas What's your name?

Anna Anna.

Tomas Where's your family? I mean, are they— [in the city?]

Anna Father: pissed off years ago. Mother: in the markets the day those big shells hit. Killed—probably—ninety-nine percent sure. Our apartment: got robbed by soldiers. Now: I need sleep so can you keep your mouth shut?

Tomas Yeah, sure, I can—

> *ANNA glares at him. TOMAS shuts up and organises his bedding.*
>
> *The light flickers and then the bulbs go out, leaving total darkness.*

Anna Told you.

Tomas What's happening?

> *ANNA switches on the party lights, powered by the car battery. They create an oddly festive coloured glow.*

Anna Ha. Party time.

> *TOMAS jumps up and tries the electric light switch.*

Tomas The power'll come back on in a sec, won't it? It can't be—

> *A bullet hits somewhere close.*
>
> *TOMAS gasps and drops to the floor.*

4

Anna Stay below window height. Don't give those bastard snipers a free shot.

TOMAS is too shaken to move.

I'll leave the lights on for a sec while you find a sleeping spot. Did you hear me? Hurry up.

Tomas Why can't you leave them on all night?

Anna Number one: can't waste battery juice. Number two: they aim for lights. Safer in the dark. Hop into bed, princess.

Tomas Don't call me that.

TOMAS turns his back on her and curls up on the floor using a curtain as a blanket. He keeps a lump of wood close by, as a weapon.

ANNA turns off the lights.

In the darkness, we hear the sound of mortars and sniper fire— some close, some distant.

Turn the lights on. Turn the lights on.

ANNA turns the lights back on.

Anna What? Ahh... scared of the dark. Where's your deadly lump of wood now, tough guy?

Tomas Shut your mouth, you—you bitch. You have to leave the lights on or I won't be able to sleep.

Anna Not my problem.

ANNA reaches to turn off the lights.

TOMAS immediately starts making some annoying noise.

Tomas I won't stop. All night.

Anna Oh! You little maggot! Hey, I worked out a good use for your weapon—I'll hit you over the head so we can both get to sleep.

Tomas Shut up! I'll punch you in the head if you come near me!

Anna You always been scared of the dark or is it just—

Tomas I'm not. I used to be—sometimes—when I was a little kid. Can't we just talk or something?

Anna Eh? Talk about what? I'm going to sleep.

She turns off the lights.

*In the darkness, we hear distant shelling and then the sound of
TOMAS trying to stifle sobs.*

ANNA groans and turns on the lights.

TOMAS doesn't want her to see him crying.

I told you, there's nothing I can do.

Tomas My mother used to read to me when I couldn't sleep.

Anna Yeah? Must've been country bumpkin paradise for you and
the goats.

She reaches to turn off the lights, then sees TOMAS's face.

I can't read to you. Just lie there *thinking* about nice things, okay?

Tomas That won't work.

Anna Oh, look… I don't know what—If I tell a story, will you shut up
and let me sleep?

Tomas What if it's a crap story?

Anna Bugger you, then. No story.

Tomas I don't know if it's a crap story until I hear it.

ANNA turns off the lights.

We hear a shaky intake of breath from TOMAS.

Anna Sshh. Don't get in a sook. Shut up and listen.

Tomas Okay.

Anna Right, well, story starts when a baby boy gets born with some
special thing so that everyone in the land knew he would grow up
to marry the king's daughter and, y'know, become the king.

Tomas What special thing? How did everyone know the baby boy
was special?

Anna Oh, I don't know. Can't remember… He had a birthmark on
his belly. Something. So—umm—the king heard about this and
didn't like the sound of it. He tricked the parents into giving him
their baby—

Tomas Why would the parents let the king take their baby?

Anna Well, let's say the king killed the parents and snatched the
baby.

Tomas Okay.

Anna The king put the baby in something—

Tomas In what?

Anna Oh look, forget the whole story thing. Just shut up and let me sleep. I can't remember every little bit of the—Oh, hang on… It was an oakwood chest… Yeah. An oak chest with shiny brass hinges and a lid carved with magnificent plum trees.

As ANNA remembers the story with some relish, a carved wooden chest is pushed into a pool of light which wells up in the darkness. It's as if the object has been conjured by ANNA's telling.

The nasty king threw the chest into the river. Down the river, a poor miller was working hard.

A MILLER appears and sees the wooden chest.

The wooden chest was just about to sink.
Miller Ooh, it might be treasure.

The MILLER fishes the chest out of the river and opens it. He carefully takes out the baby wrapped in a blanket.

Tomas But it wasn't treasure so he must've—
Anna Oh, no, I remember this bit. He was happy. The miller and his wife had longed for children for many years.

The MILLER'S WIFE appears and cuddles the baby joyfully.

Miller This is wonderful! The river has given us this great treasure.
Miller's Wife We'll take care of him as our own son!

The MILLER and his WIFE carry the baby off.

Anna He grew up to be a handsome, honest, clever boy of sixteen.

The MILLER, his WIFE and the BOY appear, all beaming happily.

There's a bit in the middle… I can't remember…

The three characters wait, stuck there, looking to ANNA for their next instruction.

Umm, I think… Oh, the miller goes off to the palace.

The MILLER grabs a travelling bundle and heads off, waving goodbye to his WIFE and the BOY.

Hang on. That's wrong.

The MILLER stops, waits for instructions.

No… of course. The boy's the one who goes off—to seek his fortune.

The MILLER comes back and hands the bundle to the BOY who gets into the idea of 'seeking his fortune'.

The MILLER and his WIFE wave goodbye.

Or maybe it's to find medicine for his sick parents…

The MILLER and his WIFE quickly change into a sick performance.

Anyway, whatever… The boy ends up at the palace and as soon as he and the princess meet, they—you know—they fall in love.

The MILLER and his WIFE disappear as the BOY travels.

He meets the PRINCESS. Flirting and in-love stuff between the BOY and the PRINCESS.

The BOY and PRINCESS pose as the young romantic couple.

Tomas Is that it? Is that the end?

Anna No, but I can't remember what—Oh! Oh, yeah, the king gets angry.

The NASTY KING appears.

Nasty King Hey! You! You must complete a noble task to prove you are worthy to marry my daughter.

Boy Okay.

Nasty King Get me three golden hairs from the head of the ogre.

Princess Father, no! Anyone who goes near the ogre is boiled up for his dinner.

The NASTY KING folds his arms. He won't budge.

Boy Well, I'll try to get the ogre's golden hairs without being eaten.

Anna The boy set off and travelled for many days.

The NASTY KING and PRINCESS vanish as the BOY trudges on valiantly.

He travelled until he reached a town where all the people were miserable and crying.

Weeping TOWNSPEOPLE appear.

The boy stopped because he was kind-hearted and didn't like to see anyone so unhappy.

Boy What's wrong?

Townswoman The tree in our town square used to bear golden plums. Now there are no golden plums or even one leaf on its branches. No one knows why.

Boy I'll try to find out.

Anna Then he travelled on to the banks of a wide river.

Boy Right… The ogre lives on that island. So how do I get across the river?

Anna There was a sad-faced ferryman who took people across.

The FERRYMAN waits with his oar as the BOY approaches.

The boy asked him…

Boy Why do you look so sad?

Tomas Because he didn't like to see anyone so unhappy.

Anna Right. Yeah.

Ferryman I am cursed to go back and forth across this river so I can never be free. No one knows how to break this curse.

Boy I'll try to find out.

The FERRYMAN disappears as the BOY steps off the boat.

Amazing… gold pieces just lying on the shore instead of sand.

Anna But the boy wasn't interested in the gold because—

Tomas He had to get the ogre's hairs.

The BOY looks up at a huge terrifying structure.

Anna Finally he arrived at the ogre's house.

Boy I think that tower is—Oh… Yes, it's built out of the bones and skulls of all the human beings he's devoured.

The BOY is terrified but steels himself to march on.

Anna The ogre wasn't home but the ogre's smelly grandmother was sitting by the fire.

The OGRE'S GRANDMOTHER plonks herself in a chair.

The boy told her his story and the old woman took pity on him.

Tomas How come? If she's an ogre's grandmother?

The OGRE'S GRANDMOTHER looks to ANNA, waiting to hear what her motivation should be.

Anna Well… she just does. That's the story. Maybe because she could see the boy was kind-hearted and honest blah blah.

The OGRE'S GRANDMOTHER shrugs and nods as if she can buy that motivation.

Ogre's Grandmother I'll help you, boy. But if the ogre finds you, he'll boil you up for his dinner. Hide behind my skirt.
Boy Thank you. By the way, why would a tree stop bringing forth golden plums? Why would the ferryman be cursed to row back and forth forever?
Ogre's Grandmother So many questions! Ssshh!
Anna Right then the ogre came home.

The BOY hides behind the OGRE'S GRANDMOTHER'S skirt as the OGRE enters.

Ogre I can smell human flesh.
Ogre's Grandmother Don't talk rubbish. You've just got the smell in your nose from last night's supper.

The OGRE grumpily scratches his head.

You've got lice again. Let me fix that for you.

The OGRE lays at his GRANDMOTHER's feet, with his head in her lap, and falls asleep.
She picks through his hair for lice.

Tomas What does she do with the lice?

The OGRE'S GRANDMOTHER waits, a louse pinched between her fingers, for instructions from ANNA.

Anna She eats them.

The OGRE'S GRANDMOTHER pops the louse in her mouth.

Tomas Errgghh… Yes.
Anna When the ogre had fallen asleep, the grandmother pulled out one of the golden hairs from his head.

The OGRE'S GRANDMOTHER does that, making the OGRE wake with a yelp.

Ogre Ow!

Ogre's Grandmother Sorry, I fell asleep and had a bad dream about a tree that used to bear golden plums but now is barren.

Ogre Ha! That's my doing! I put a rat down to gnaw at the root of that tree. Until the rat is killed, there'll be no golden plums. Now let me sleep or I'll thump you.

The OGRE falls to snoring again.

Anna The old woman pulled out two more of his golden hairs.

Ogre Ow! Another bad dream?

Anna Oh, hang on, I forgot the other question the boy has to—

Tomas The ferryman.

Anna Oh, yeah.

The OGRE growls and raises his fist to his GRANDMOTHER.

Ogre's Grandmother Don't get your undies in a twist. It's not my fault I had a bad dream about a ferryman cursed to go back and forth forever.

Ogre Oh, that guy. He annoyed me once. But all that fool has to do is put the oar into another man's hand and he would be free.

Dean Mason as the Ogre and Claudia Tory as the Ogre's Grandmother in the 2007 atyp production. (Photo: Allan Vella)

Anna Finally the grandmother let the ogre sleep. In the morning, the ogre went out—

Tomas Hunting for human flesh!

Anna I guess so, yeah.

> *The OGRE wakes up, grumbles about his hungry belly and exits. The BOY reappears from behind the OGRE'S GRANDMOTHER's skirt.*

Ogre's Grandmother Here are the three golden hairs you need and you have the answers to your two questions.

Boy Thank you.

> *The BOY meets the FERRYMAN.*

Anna On his way back, the boy had an answer for the ferryman.

Boy I know the secret of how to break the curse!

> *The BOY whispers the secret to the FERRYMAN and then waves him goodbye.*

Good luck!

Anna He travelled on to the town with the barren tree.

> *The BOY meets the TOWNSPEOPLE again.*

He had the answer the townspeople needed.

Townswoman Yes, it worked! We've killed that rat—

Boy And now your tree is covered in golden plums again!

Townswoman How can we ever thank you? Please, please take this chest full of gold as our thanks!

Boy Are you sure? Great!

Anna Back at the palace…

> *The BOY drags on a chest of gold and then bows before the NASTY KING.*

Boy Here are the ogre's three golden hairs.

> *The NASTY KING isn't interested in the ogre's hairs. He's too busy drooling over the chests full of gold.*

Nasty King Where did you get all this gold?

Boy On that island, gold lies on the shore instead of sand. Just let the ferryman take you across in his boat.

Anna The gold-hungry king went straight to the river.

The NASTY KING breathlessly runs up to the FERRYMAN.

Nasty King Row me across to the island!

Anna The ferryman put the oar in the king's hand and ran away.

The FERRYMAN whoops for joy.

Ferryman I'm free. But from now on, you'll be cursed to row back and forth with no escape.

We see the cursed NASTY KING wretchedly rowing.

We see the BOY, wearing a crown, embracing the PRINCESS, the MILLER and his WIFE.

Anna The boy married the princess and became king—the wisest, kindest king the land had ever known.

Tomas The end.

Anna Yeah. The end of the only story I can think of.

Tomas That's a long story to remember in your head.

Anna My grandmother must've told me different versions of it four thousand times.

Tomas It was your favourite.

Anna Don't know. Must've been.

Tomas Where is she now?

Anna Who?

Tomas Your grandmother.

Anna Dead. Are you gonna shut up and sleep now?

Tomas Maybe.

Anna Either way, just shut up.

ANNA turns away and curls up to sleep.

Eyes fluttering with sleepiness, TOMAS focuses on the rowing KING, the BOY with the PRINCESS, etc.

As TOMAS sinks into sleep, the light fades and the story characters are swallowed up in the darkness.

Scene Two

The house. Daytime.

TOMAS wakes up suddenly and scrambles to his feet, uncertain where he is for a moment.

Tomas Anna?

There's no sign of her.

Scene Three

City streets. Daytime.

TOMAS walks through the city, clutching a street map, anxious. He finds PEOPLE on the end of a queue.

Tomas Excuse me. What is this queue for?

Man/Woman 1 Supposed to be food hand-outs here today. [*Laughing*] But I'm beginning to think two people happened to stand in a line and—whoosh—a rumour got going. So maybe we're all standing here for no reason.

Tomas [*indicating on his street map*] Can you tell me how to get here?

Man/Woman 1 The police station? Why?

Tomas Well, my parents always said—

Man/Woman 1 There's nothing there anymore.

Tomas Oh… then… where are people supposed to go if they get separated from their families and need to—I'm not from here. We're from the south—

Man/Woman 1 Then you should go home.

Tomas I can't go home. Isn't there someone I can—I mean—?

Another WOMAN in the queue moans and sways.

Woman 2 They're all gone. All gone. All gone.

WOMAN 2 is crying and swaying, freaking TOMAS out.

Man/Woman 1 [*to WOMAN 2*] Ssh. Ssh.

But TOMAS is too unnerved by the moaning WOMAN to stick around.

He backs away and then runs off. He's out of breath, not sure where to go.

He spots a MAN wearing a uniform jacket. The MAN is picking through the rubble to find cigarette butts which he collects in a plastic cup.

Tomas Excuse me! Are you police? Can you help me?

The MAN IN THE JACKET turns and laughs.

Man in the Jacket   Parking officer. See? [*He points to an insignia on his jacket.*] Except I'm not even a real parking officer. It's just a good jacket.

A sniper bullet whizzes close by.

The MAN IN THE JACKET dives behind something but TOMAS is frozen, overwhelmed.

Get down, kid! You want to get your head blown off?

TOMAS dives low against a wall and crawls away, terrified.

In another street, a MAN sits with a few tins of sardines in front of him.

ANNA is holding out a cigarette lighter.

Anna   Come on. Make it two tins.

Sardine Man   [*shaking his head*] These are worth more now there's no power. You can eat sardines straight, no cooking required.

Anna   This is a new lighter. Packet not even opened. It's a good deal.

The SARDINE MAN shakes his head.

ANNA makes a show of walking away, until the SARDINE MAN whistles and reluctantly holds up two tins.

ANNA exchanges them for the lighter. She slips them into her plastic bags and hurries off.

TOMAS wanders along a street. The shelling intensifies with people running for shelter around him. When a shell explodes nearby, TOMAS flinches but doesn't know where to go.

An oddly CHEERFUL MAN runs past, diving for shelter behind rubble.

Cheerful Man   Watch out, mate! They're doing their target practice here this arvo.

The CHEERFUL MAN tugs at TOMAS's trouser leg until he drops down to safety.

The CHEERFUL MAN grins as he and TOMAS catch their breath behind the rubble.

Sniper bullets zing past them.

Whoo! That one was close! Amazing how you get used to things. A few months ago, I was shitting my pants to have bullets fired at my head. But then you're so sick of being scared all day every day, you get sort of numb to it.

Tomas Umm... I think I get what you mean.

Cheerful Man You all right, mate? You look a bit wobbly. Are you right for somewhere to stay? If you're hungry, maybe—

> *A bullet hits the CHEERFUL MAN and he slumps back against the rubble.*
>
> *TOMAS touches him gingerly, not sure if he's dead.*
>
> *A WOMAN runs past and shelters nearby.*

Tomas Excuse me... he's been shot. I'm not sure if he's—

Woman 3 Is this your father?

Tomas No.

> *The WOMAN dashes across and checks the CHEERFUL MAN.*

Woman 3 There's a resemblance. Looks like he could be your father.

Tomas Why would I say he wasn't my father if he really was? My father's—I don't know—but—

Woman 3 Well, he's dead, whoever he is.

Tomas Oh...

Woman 3 Hey, I wouldn't lounge around here.

Tomas We should carry him somewhere.

Woman 3 Too dangerous right now. You'd better get out of here.

> *The WOMAN runs off.*
>
> *TOMAS tries to get a hold on the body to carry it but it's heavy and the sniper fire doesn't let up. He manages to drag it a few metres but then the body of the CHEERFUL MAN falls against him. TOMAS shudders and extricates himself.*
>
> *He dives across to another sheltered spot. He dry retches, gulping for air.*
>
> *People drag the body of the CHEERFUL MAN offstage as TOMAS runs off.*

Scene Four

The house. Night.

There's just the coloured glow from the party lights.

TOMAS is hunched up in a corner, shaken from the day, bewildered.
ANNA is sorting the bags of things she's scrounged. She opens a tin of
sardines and starts eating them from the tin with a fork.

Anna I can't believe I've got carrot-boy for another night.

> *She's aware TOMAS is watching her hungrily.*

You scrounged some food today, didn't you?

Tomas Some.

Anna You ever touch any of my stuff, I'll rip you apart.

Tomas I didn't.

Anna Look, you've got to trade for things you want.

Tomas I haven't got anything to… Only what was in my pockets
when the soldiers came. This penknife.

> *He slides a penknife across the floor. ANNA examines it, then*
> *scoops it up.*
> *She slides the other tin of sardines across to him.*
> *TOMAS opens the tin and eats.*

Anna Phew… Princess, you stink. I can smell you from here.

Tomas It's my clothes.

Anna Wash them.

Tomas These are my only clothes. Do you want me to sit here nude
while I wait for them to dry?

Anna Erghh… No thank you. I'd rather put up with the stink than
be forced to look at your dangly giblets. Find out anything about
your family today?

> *TOMAS shakes his head, fighting tears.*

Yeah, well, it's a bit of a mess out there.

> *TOMAS wipes his eyes, not wanting her to see him upset.*

I'm turning the lights off now.

Tomas Leave them on.

Anna Oh God, more scared-of-the-dark blubbing from carrot-boy.

> *TOMAS starts doing the annoying noise.*

Aahh! We can't leave the lights on—can you get that through
your mashed-potato brain?

TOMAS turns his back on her. ANNA can see he's really shaky.

You were okay last night, weren't you?

TOMAS shrugs, his back turned to her.

Look, what if I do another story and you—?
Tomas You said you could only remember one.
Anna Well, I think I can remember another one. One my mad uncle used to tell. But no lights on. That's the deal.

TOMAS is about to argue but ANNA glares at him and he shrugs, reluctantly.

He curls up in his makeshift bed as ANNA turns out the party lights.

At first there's darkness as we hear her voice.

Okay. The story's called 'Lazy Gus'. Lazy Gus was one of the greatest bludgers the world has ever seen.

In a pool of light, LAZY GUS appears, lolling on something.

People in the town were used to seeing Lazy Gus slob around all day.

TOWNSPEOPLE shake their heads with disapproval.

Townsperson 1 He's too lazy to get a job.
Townsperson 2 He's too lazy even to wash.
Townsperson 1 He smells of cheesy old socks.

The TOWNSPEOPLE screw their noses up at the smell.

Townsperson 2 Lazy Gus is no use at all to his poor hungry wife and poor hungry kids.

GUS'S WIFE trudges past, carrying a baby in a bundle.

LAZY GUS shrugs to her—what can I do?—and wanders away.

Anna One day, Lazy Gus felt hungry, so he pinched a cooked chicken from Mrs Brown's kitchen table.

LAZY GUS wanders on, chomping on a chicken leg.

Gus was too lazy to chew properly, so a chicken bone got stuck in his throat.

LAZY GUS starts choking, writhing on the ground.

Tomas What happens? Does he—?

Anna He dies.

LAZY GUS has one last choking spasm and dies.

Tomas Far out. Okay.

Anna Mrs Brown found Lazy Gus dead on her back porch.

MRS BROWN rushes in and checks the body.

Mrs Brown Oh no! People might think I poisoned Lazy Gus for stealing my chicken. I don't want to hang for murder.

MRS BROWN drags the body of LAZY GUS away.

Anna Mrs Brown carried Lazy Gus down to the river.

She leans the body against something and props a fishing rod in his hand. She checks no one has seen her and then runs away.

At dawn the next day, a fisherman went down to the river.

The FISHERMAN enters with his fishing rod and spots LAZY GUS.

Fisherman Morning, Lazy Gus! Getting any bites? It's not like you to be up and about this early. Good on you!

He waits for a response from LAZY GUS.

Gus? I said 'good on you'.

Still no response.

No need to be rude. Are you too lazy to say hello now? Oy!

The FISHERMAN prods LAZY GUS with his fishing rod. The limp body topples forward.

Anna The body of Lazy Gus fell into the river and was quickly swept away under the water.

The FISHERMAN runs along the river bank, trying to grab hold of LAZY GUS.

Fisherman Sorry, mate! Grab onto the fishing rod! I'll pull you out!

Anna Half a kilometre downstream, the fisherman finally managed to pull Lazy Gus out of the water.

The FISHERMAN hoists him out of the river.

Fisherman He's dead! Bloody hell, I don't want people to know I drowned Lazy Gus.

Anna The fisherman dried off Lazy Gus and propped him up against Farmer Jones' stable door.

The FISHERMAN drags the body to the stable door and props it up. Then he sneaks away.

It just so happened that Farmer Jones was on the lookout for the thief who'd stolen his best horse the week before.

FARMER JONES appears, patrolling with his gun.

Tomas Oh, so when he sees Lazy Gus—

Farmer Jones You! Move away from the stable door or I'll shoot!

LAZY GUS doesn't move.

I mean it! I'll shoot! One, two, three...

He fires his gun and the body slumps sideways.
FARMER JONES rushes over.

Tomas But he must have realised—

Anna Wait for it.

Farmer Jones Oh... it's Lazy Gus. He's too lazy to be a horse thief. And now I've shot him dead! I don't want to hang for murder.

Anna So Farmer Jones lifted Lazy Gus onto his second-best horse and tied him into the saddle.

One or two performers play the horse, trotting on stage to have LAZY GUS tied on its back.

He sent the horse running down the main street of the town.

FARMER JONES chases after the horse.

Farmer Jones Thief! A thief has stolen my horse! Someone stop him!

Anna The townspeople came rushing out of their houses, throwing rocks at the thief.

Various TOWNSPEOPLE call to him to stop, hurling rocks.

Tomas So now all those people think they'd killed him.

Anna Exactly. Finally, they caught the horse and discovered that the rider was Lazy Gus and he was dead.

The body of LAZY GUS is carried on stage with various characters attending in sombre funeral mode.

At his funeral, Mrs Brown passed around a collection bucket for the poor hungry widow and orphans. All the people who thought they'd killed Lazy Gus were feeling horribly guilty. So they put heaps of money in the collection bucket.

People empty their pockets into the bucket.

MRS BROWN hands the bucket to LAZY GUS'S WIFE. She is astonished by the pile of gold coins or cash.

Mrs Brown There's enough money for you and your children to live in comfort for the rest of your lives.

Townsperson 1 So in the end, Lazy Gus did some good for his poor wife and kids.

Townsperson 2 As a dead man.

Most of the TOWNSPEOPLE exit.

Anna That one appeals to people with a sicko sense of humour.

Tomas Yeah. It was good.

Anna Reckon you'll be okay to sleep?

Tomas Dunno. Maybe.

Anna Goodnight, then.

ANNA goes to sleep.

TOMAS lies there watching MRS BROWN, the FISHERMAN and FARMER JONES sneak over to the coffin of LAZY GUS and whisper 'I'm sorry', one by one.

TOMAS curls up to sleep as the the body of LAZY GUS is carried off for burial.

Tomas Anna?

Anna Oh, what is it now?

Tomas Nothing.

Anna Hey, potato-face, did you check at the railway station today?

Tomas What? The railway station?

Anna No trains going anywhere of course—but on the wall by the clock there's a place where people leave messages.

Tomas Messages?

Anna Notes with information about family, friends, whatever. You could look there.

Tomas Do you look for messages on the wall?

Anna Who from? No, I'm okay. I'm just waiting till those maniacs run out of bombs and I can go back to our apartment.

Tomas Oh, right. Be good to go home.

Anna Sleep now.

Tomas Yeah. Goodnight.

Scene Five

Daytime. The street outside Anna's apartment building.

ANNA stares across the street in shock and sinks down to sit on the gutter.

A WOMAN comes past, dragging something she's scrounged. She notices ANNA.

Woman Neighbour It burned down yesterday.

Anna I didn't know.

Woman Neighbour Oh, I know you… You lived in an apartment on the middle floor. You and your mother, yeah?

Anna I was going to move back once—

Woman Neighbour Find some other empty apartment.

Anna Twelve years we lived here and when our apartment got looted, the neighbours didn't do one thing to help us.

Woman Neighbour Well, people are afraid.

Anna Some of the bastard neighbours stole our things themselves.

Woman Neighbour That's how things are now.

Anna But our family papers, birth certificates, our photos—my mother had them taped behind the kitchen cupboards.

Woman Neighbour Your papers and photos would all be burnt up now, lovey.

> *ANNA nods numbly.*

Count yourself lucky you weren't still living there. Some of the people didn't get out.

Scene Six

Daytime. The railway station.

TOMAS faces a wall covered in photos and scraps of paper—different colours and sizes—stuck on there. He goes closer to read some of the notes.

There are a few other people looking at the notes or hanging around, waiting, including a STATION GUARD.

Station Guard Hunting for something in particular?

Tomas My family.

Station Guard Look for your family name on the front. Or the name of someone you know.

Tomas What do the notes say?

Station Guard Read some if you want.

Tomas Oh… But is it okay to read a message written for someone else?

Station Guard Who here is going to arrest you? Not me.

> *TOMAS scans the notes on the wall.*

See those people waiting? In their notes, they set a time to wait here every day. [*He indicates the big clock.*] 'I promise to be here such and such a time.'

> *TOMAS continues looking at the notes while the STATION GUARD raves on to the other people waiting…*

Promises. Yes, well, a lot of promises have been broken in this country. The internationals have gone. We're on our own now.

> *The other people nod in grim agreement.*
>
> *TOMAS plucks one of the notes off the wall.*

Tomas This name… There was a family with this name in our district.

Station Guard Well, read it. If there's a chance you'll find out something, read it.

> *TOMAS peeks inside the note.*

Tomas Yes! I do know this family. They lived just down the road from…

> *As TOMAS reads, he's increasingly shaken.*

23

Station Guard And?

Tomas This note wasn't meant for me. I should put it back.

> *TOMAS reaches to stick the note back up.*
> *The STATION GUARD takes it from him and reads it.*

Station Guard Ah, the father taken into the woods. Shot.

> *TOMAS snatches the note from the STATION GUARD's hand and sticks it back up. He doesn't want to know about it.*

Half of these notes, it's bad news—'your son is dead', 'your sister was killed'. And the rest… most of these people will never be found.

> *TOMAS doesn't want to see or hear any more. He runs past the STATION GUARD and out.*

Scene Seven

Night. The house.

By the glow of the party lights, TOMAS and ANNA are eating food out of foil packets.

Anna This is like eating congealed floor dust. Is this the best you could find?

Tomas I didn't know it would be this disgusting.

Anna Hey, cabbage-head, I found some—

Tomas Don't call me that.

Anna Actually I wish you were a cabbage. I could make soup out of you.

Tomas I wish I was a potato-head.

Anna Yes. Potato would be better.

Tomas Then we could make mashed potato dripping with heaps of butter.

Anna Oh, stop. Don't even say it.

> *ANNA and TOMAS moan with food-lust and then laugh.*

I had some good finds today.

> *She pulls items out of the plastic bags.*

Clean clothes for the stinky farm boy.

> *ANNA hands TOMAS a pile of folded clothes.*

24

Tomas I don't get it. You have different moods like, whoosh—total bitch one second and then whoosh—nice the next second.

Anna Oh well, sixteen-year-old girls do that. We're supposed to be moody.

Tomas You said you were a hundred and five.

Anna I am. But also sixteen.

Tomas That's stupid. You can't—

Anna You understand nothing. I used to be sixteen. I'd picked out what senior subjects I was going to do. I got top marks at school, you know.

Tomas Well, maybe later, you can—

Anna Anyway, I'm not being *nice* to you. I just can't stand the smell. The stink of you would kill a goat. Get changed.

TOMAS goes behind something to change his clothes.

[*Laughing*] Come over all modest have we, princess?

Tomas Shut up.

Anna Promise I won't peek. The last thing I want to see is your—

Tomas My dangly giblets. I know.

While TOMAS changes, ANNA keeps talking.

Anna I went to our old apartment building today. It was burned to the ground.

Tomas What? Your house is gone? What will you do now?

Anna Maybe I don't want to stay in this maggoty hole of a city much longer anyway.

Tomas Where would you go? How will you get out? Everyone reckons—

Anna I've been sussing things out. Apparently, people with foreign relatives can get on special buses and across the border. My great grandfather was French which makes my mother quarter French. Which means we could live in a proper country until things get okay again here.

TOMAS emerges in the clean clothes.
ANNA does a swooning, you-look-wonderful act.

Oh, carrot boy! I never realised—

Tomas You say one more word and I'll—

25

Anna Yeah, yeah.

TOMAS goes back to his foil food packet.

Some of our old neighbours were killed in the fire.

Tomas Maybe it was punishment because they didn't help you before.

Anna What?

Tomas I mean, the reason they got killed was because they—

Anna People don't get killed for any reason. There's no reason.

Tomas I thought it would feel like revenge for you.

Anna It doesn't work that way.

Tomas I want revenge.

ANNA looks at him, hearing the hard tone.

Anna Revenge against who?

Tomas The guys who broke into our house wore black ski masks. But one of them—I recognised his voice. His kids go to my school. We played soccer, we went to each other's houses. The men in the ski masks kept hitting my dad.

Anna Nothing you can do about it now.

Tomas I want to rip the ski masks off their disgusting faces and smash them into the wall.

TOMAS's angry energy crumbles into tears. He turns away from ANNA, not wanting her to see.

If you turn the lights off right now I'll smash your face into the wall.

ANNA lets a silence go, then reaches into a plastic bag.

Anna Check out what I found today. *Folk Tales from Many Lands.*

TOMAS turns to look at the big old book she's holding.

Tomas Give us a look.

Anna Not now. I'm not wasting battery power so you can read when it's dark.

Tomas Just for tonight, can't you please—?

Anna No. Before you start whining—I had a read of one of the stories today. I could tell it you.

Tomas Oh...

Anna It's that or nothing.

ANNA turns out the lights.

Story's called 'The Singing Bones'.

Tomas Bones singing? What? Why?

Anna Listen. A long time ago, back in the days when dogs wore feathered hats to walk down the street, long before our great great grandfathers who are now dead were even born—

Tomas You got that from the book?

Anna Yeah. I kind of liked it. Shoosh and listen. Way back then, there was a king who was struck down with mysterious blindness. The finest doctors tried to cure him.

In a pool of light we see a KING being examined by a DOCTOR.

Doctor The only cure is from the feather of the silver bird.

Anna So the king called for his two sons.

King Serge! Peter!

The two princes, SERGE and PETER, appear and kneel before the blind KING.

My sons, I want you to travel to that distant forest and find the silver bird. Whoever brings back a silver feather to cure my blindness will have my crown.

Anna So the two princes travelled to the distant forest.

We see the two princes searching the forest.

SERGE thunders through the forest, aiming a bow and arrow, while PETER carefully looks around.

Peter, the younger brother, was a nice guy and smart. He stayed very quiet and still until the silver bird landed on a branch.

Peter Hey, little silver bird. I won't hurt you.

He gently picks up the bird and strokes it.

Would you mind if I took just one of your silver feathers?

Anna The bird let Peter pluck out one of its silver feathers.

SERGE is watching PETER with the bird.

The older brother, Serge, was pretty sulky and, y'know, a bit of a bully.

SERGE aims his bow at the bird.

Peter   No, brother! I already have the feather!

SERGE fires an arrow into the bird.

Anna   The arrow struck and the beautiful silver bird vanished forever.

Tomas   But at least they got the feather.

Anna   Yes, but wait. As the two brothers travelled home, Serge became jealous.

Serge   [*angrily to himself*] Now Peter's going to get the crown. No, no, no, I can't let that happen. I should be the next king.

Anna   Serge pushed Peter into a fast-flowing river.

SERGE pushes PETER into the river.

Peter   Brother! Please help me!

PETER reaches out for help but SERGE holds his brother's head under the water until he goes limp.

He tries to get the feather out of PETER's hand but fails.

Anna   Peter was drowned. And the silver feather was lost in the swirling water. Back at the palace, Serge put on a good act.

We see SERGE fall weeping at the feet of the blind KING.

Serge   Oh, father, we failed to get a feather because Peter shot the silver bird.

King   And where is your younger brother?

Serge   On our way home, he fell into a raging river. I tried to save him but alas…

SERGE breaks down, unable to go on.

The KING reaches to comfort him.

Then the KING takes the crown off his head and puts it on SERGE.

Tomas   Is that it? He gets away with it? Gets away with killing his brother and no one ever knows? What a crap ending—a person does something terrible and the world doesn't even find out.

Anna   No. I was pausing for dramatic effect.

Tomas   Well, it wasn't dramatic. It sounded like that was the end.

ANNA growls at him.

Sorry. Keep going.

Anna Many years passed but the blind king was still torn up about the death of his son. And Serge felt terribly guilty.

SERGE tries to comfort the wretched blind KING.

Serge Father, I will find musicians to come and play to give you comfort. I'll bring the best from every land, no matter how much it costs me.

Anna Two of these great musicians travelled from beyond the distant forest.

Two MUSICIANS trudge along, carrying various instruments.

As they passed the raging river, something white washed up on the bank.

One MUSICIAN finds a white bone and reaches down, drawn to its special power.

Musician 1 You know, this bone would make a very good flute.

The other MUSICIAN, also spellbound, picks up another white bone.

Musician 2 And this breastbone—I could fashion it into a new lute.

Anna The two musos drilled holes and added strings and whatever you do to turn human bones into instruments.

The KING lolls in a chair wretchedly.

Serge Here are new musicians, father, to bring you some comfort.

The MUSICIANS enter with their bone instruments.
As soon as one puts the flute to his lips and plays, a voice is heard calling out along with the music.

Flute / Peter's Voice Father! It's me, your son Peter!

MUSICIAN 1 stops, surprised. MUSICIAN 2 plays the lute.

Lute / Peter's Voice My brother killed the silver bird with his arrow.

Serge What's going on? Stop playing! Those instruments must be enchanted. Stop!

SERGE goes to snatch the instruments away but the KING holds SERGE back with a firm hand.

King Let them play. Let's hear the truth.

Flute / Peter's Voice My brother drowned me in the river.

Lute / Peter's Voice I was murdered and my bones washed clean by the raging water.

Flute / Peter's Voice My bones now lie in the crystal pool.

King Go to this crystal pool immediately! I want the rest of Peter's bones brought back. My son should have a proper burial.

The DOCTOR hurries off to do this.

Lute / Peter's Voice And in the crystal pool you'll find a silver feather too.

The DOCTOR returns with the silver feather.

Anna That silver feather cured the king's blindness.

Tomas What about Serge? The murdering one?

Anna Yeah, well, Serge felt so guilty now the truth was out, he ran to the highest tower and threw himself off to a bone-shattering

From left: Dean Mason as the King, Kyle Hedrick as the Doctor and Tyrone Lindqvist as Serge in the 2007 atyp production. (Photo: Allan Vella)

death. From that day on, the king kept the musicians always by his side, so he could hear his son's voice in the singing bones.

The light begins to fade on the KING and the MUSICIANS.

Tomas I like that one.

Anna Yeah.

Tomas We could find other stories in that book.

Anna Well, I don't know how long I'll be hanging around. The special buses—

Tomas Right. Yeah. Well, good luck.

Anna Did you have any luck at the railway station? Any messages from your family or—?

Tomas No. It creeped me out, that place. But now I'm thinking—I don't know—I should write a note. In case my family go there.

Anna It's worth a try.

ANNA finds paper and a pencil and hands them to TOMAS.
She turns up the party lights.

Tomas What would I write?

Anna 'Dear Mum and Dad, this is Tomas. I'm alive. I hope you're alive too.'

TOMAS starts scribbling the note.

Tomas I'll put a meeting time. 'I promise to wait at the railway station at two o'clock every day.'

Anna Yep. Not as stupid as you look.

TOMAS tucks the note in his pocket.

The minute I figure out how to get across the border I'm—The point is, don't be surprised if I'm suddenly gone.

Tomas Oh, sure. Once my family—I mean, I'll be heading off too.

TOMAS wanders around the room, restless.

I hope they see my note.

Anna Shut up, carrot-boy. Sleep.

ANNA turns off the lights.

END OF ACT ONE

31

ACT TWO

Scene One

Daytime. The house.
Some of Tomas's clothes are drying on a line. The camp is more established, with garden chairs, a spare car battery, etc.
TOMAS sits, reading the book of folktales.
ANNA enters, carting her bags of booty.

Anna You hungry?
Tomas Always.

>*ANNA chucks him a small tin.*

Anna There was an aid van handing these out. I don't think I can sell them for much so let's call it lunch.

>*ANNA and TOMAS peel the tops off the tins and eat the contents with forks.*

You been reading?
Tomas Which one are you going to do tonight? What about 'The Toad Bridegroom'?
Anna I've done that twice already.
Tomas What about 'The Goblin's Eggs' or the one about the dog and the—
Anna No. I might look at some new ones this afternoon.

>*ANNA slips the book into her scavenging bag.*

Tomas What is this stuff we're eating?
Anna I'm guessing meat.

>*TOMAS peers at the writing on the side of the tin.*

Tomas But what kind of meat? This is written in a weirdo language.
Anna Other side. It's got different languages.

>*They read the other side of the tins.*

Oh my God, one of the ingredients is 'beef lips'.

Tomas You're making that up. It can't—Oh, yeah! 'Beef lips.'

They laugh and spit out the mouthfuls they've got.

Anna You don't think about cows having meaty lips.

Tomas Yummo.

Anna [*eating more from the tin*] Mmm, tender, juicy cow lips. God, how lucky are we.

TOMAS laughs and joins her in eating with exaggerated delight.

Tomas Ooh, no, actually we are lucky. Check out what I got this morning.

He reaches into his jacket and reveals something with a flourish.

Condensed milk!

He tips his head back and drinks a gulp of condensed milk.
ANNA grabs the tin from him.

Anna Give us a go.

She takes a big mouthful.

Tomas Good, eh.

Anna Mmm, yeah.

Tomas Hey, don't be a pig with it.

Reluctantly, ANNA hands back the tin.

Anna Let's save the rest for tonight.

Tomas You're right. Make it last.

He sneaks one last gulp.
ANNA roars with mock outrage but they are both laughing.
He puts the tin away.

Anna Turn your back.

TOMAS obediently turns his back while ANNA retrieves something from a hiding spot. She brings out a pendant on a chain.

Amber. Do you even know what amber is, carrot-boy? It's sap from a tree from millions of years ago. See inside? A bee. Trapped inside the amber, perfect, even though it's millions of years old.

ANNA lets TOMAS reach out to touch the amber pendant.

I'm going to sell it today.

Tomas What? What for?

ANNA puts the chain around her neck with the pendant tucked inside her bra.

Anna I heard about a guy who forges papers. I have to get some American dollars from somewhere. Hey—did you realise it's nearly two o'clock?

Tomas What!? I'm gonna be late.

Anna You better get back to the railway station.

TOMAS scrambles to get his shoes on and rushes out the door.

Scene Two

Daytime. Street.

A BLACKMARKET WOMAN examines the amber pendant hanging around ANNA's neck.

Blackmarket Woman That's it. That's my final offer.

Anna Come on, it's worth heaps more. A valuable antique. Belonged to my mother, before that my grandmother, before that—

Blackmarket Woman Can you eat it or burn it for fuel to cook dinner?

Anna No.

Blackmarket Woman Look, honey, if it's a family treasure, you should just keep it.

Anna This isn't the time to be soppy about pretty shiny things.

Blackmarket Woman That's why I can only offer you a few American dollars for this.

Anna Don't bullshit me. If no one wants this stuff, why would you buy it?

Blackmarket Woman Because one day the world will crawl its way back to normal and people will pay for pretty shiny things again.

The BLACKMARKET WOMAN plays it cool, maybe checks

through her sports bag of tradeable goods.

ANNA sighs and presses the pendant to her skin one last time. Then she takes it off and hands it to the WOMAN.

While the WOMAN counts out cash, ANNA blabs on defiantly…

Anna With these American dollars, I'll get across the border. My great grandfather was French. So I'll be allowed to live there. I think I'll live in Paris.

Scene Three

Daytime. Railway station.

The STATION GUARD stands by the message wall. TOMAS hurries in, breathless.

Station Guard No need to panic, son. No one has turned up hunting for you.

Tomas Oh. Right, okay. I'm just going to wait here. Two hours. Like it says in my note.

Station Guard Try looking along there. A few new ones have gone up.

> *TOMAS checks the new messages. He spots one and plucks it off the wall.*

A message for you?

Tomas That's my name.

Station Guard Then it's for you.

> *TOMAS holds the note but doesn't turn it over. His hand shakes.*

Is there a problem?

Tomas I don't know…

Station Guard Afraid that this message has bad news?

> *TOMAS nods.*

Would you like me to read it to you?

> *TOMAS hands him the note.*
>
> *The STATION GUARD indicates the writing on the front of the note.*

This is you? And this person is—

35

Tomas A friend of my brother.

Station Guard 'Tomas, Last week, I saw your brother Nick. He was all right. If I see him again, I'll tell him to go to the railway station to find you. Best wishes.'

TOMAS takes the note from the STATION GUARD and stares at it.

Scene Four

Daytime. Street.

ANNA enters, carrying large empty plastic containers. She joins a queue of people carrying similar containers.

Anna Is the queue moving fast or slow?

Woman in Water Queue I've been here one hour and I've moved this far.

She demonstrates a distance of a couple of metres.

Anna Oh, well, I won't be queueing up for water much longer. I'm getting out. Get myself to a country where water comes out of the taps like it's supposed to.

Woman in Water Queue Getting out how?

Anna There are buses that take people—

Woman in Water Queue Oh no, the buses have stopped. Two days ago.

Anna What? No, this is for people with relatives from—

Woman in Water Queue No, no—haven't you heard? That's all finished since they bombed the bridge.

Man in Water Queue Dead right. Blockades on every road. No vehicles are getting out now.

The queue moves forward but ANNA stands there, crushed.

Woman in Water Queue Don't lose your place in the line.

Anna I don't know what I should—I don't know if… I have to work out what to do now…

Woman in Water Queue Now, you're queuing for water.

There's a renewed barrage of shelling and the people in the water queue scatter, running for shelter.

ANNA struggles to run with the water containers. She's on the verge of tears.

Around her people are running back and forth to escape sniper fire and mortars.

ANNA takes shelter behind rubble and tries to catch her breath.

She notices a WOMAN in a distinctive blue coat.

Anna Mum... Mum?

The WOMAN in the coat runs a few metres on, away from ANNA.

Mum! Mum! Wait! Mum! It's me!

ANNA dumps the water containers and runs after the WOMAN. The WOMAN is focused on finding a safe spot and doesn't notice ANNA until she grabs her shoulder.

Mum! It's me—Anna!

The WOMAN turns around and ANNA's face instantly falls.

Woman in Coat Anna. It's good to see you're safe. Where have you—?

The WOMAN registers the look on ANNA's face.

Oh, sweetheart, did you think—?

ANNA can't speak.

The coat. Yes, this is your mum's coat. She left it in the staffroom. I went to your apartment to find you. I left messages there.

Anna They burnt it down.

Woman in Coat Where've you been living?

Anna I saw her coat. I thought—

Woman in Coat I'm sorry. I thought you knew about your mum.

Anna I did know—Well, I wasn't...

Woman in Coat You couldn't help hoping.

The WOMAN reaches to embrace her. ANNA backs away, shaking.

She was a few metres away from me in the market. She was—Listen, we can't talk properly here. It's not safe. Come with me—

But ANNA is wandering away, overcome.

Do you want the coat? It's warm. It'll be winter soon and you'll need it.

>ANNA shakes her head and runs off, leaving the water containers.

Scene Five

Night. The house.

TOMAS is huddled up next to the party lights, reading the folktales book.

The sound of mortar shells is relentless.

The battery is running low, making the lights too dim, so he gives up and closes the book.

TOMAS hears a noise near the doorway.

Tomas Anna! How come you're so late? I started getting really worried a couple of hours ago. I even—

>*He hears another noise.*

Anna? Is that you?

>*TOMAS nervously shifts around so he can see what made the noise.*

Oh… hey, pussycat.

>*TOMAS tries to entice the cat into the room.*

Here, puss puss puss. Okay then, don't. We don't want you sniffing around here stealing our beef lips.

>*He shoos the cat away.*

>*TOMAS listens again. There's nothing but the sound of the mortars.*

>*He fiddles with the wires connecting the lights to the battery but there's little power left.*

>*He nods off, then shakes himself awake, slapping his face. But a moment later, he falls asleep.*

>*The semi-darkness is cut by a torch beam.*

>*ANNA enters. She's shaken, filthy, with blood on her clothes. She's been bashed around the face, scratched and bloody.*

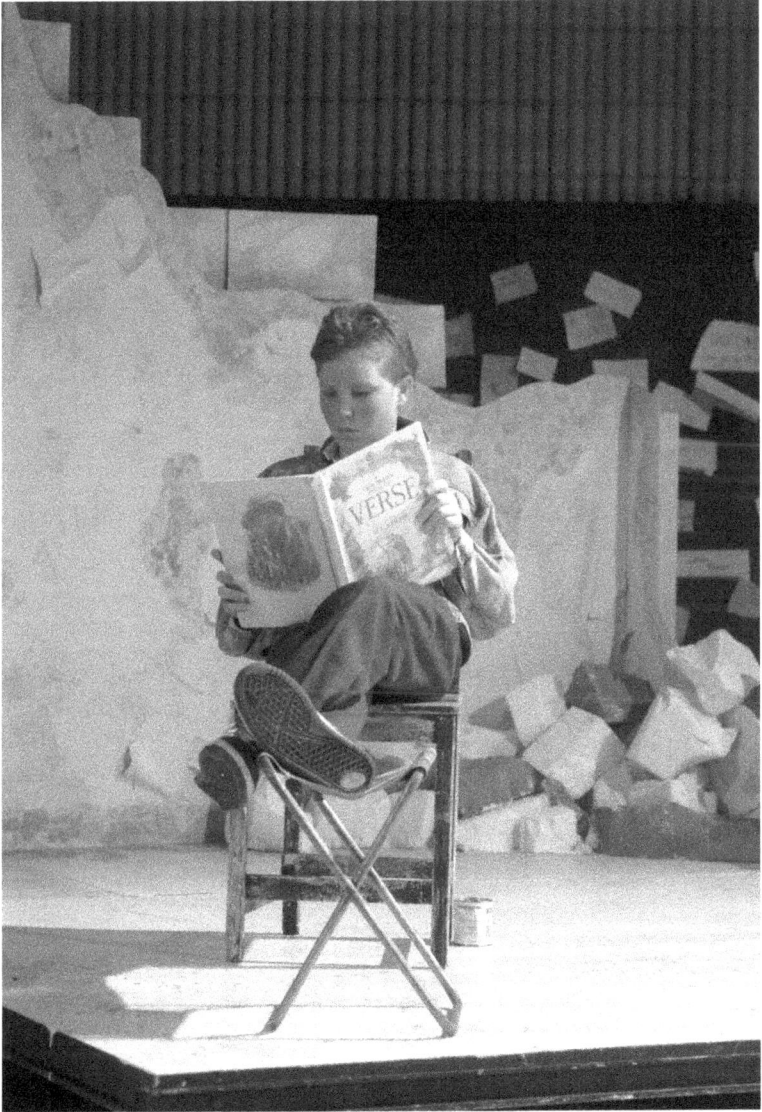

Cooper Torrens as Tomas in the 2007 atyp production.
(Photo: Allan Vella)

Anna Have you run the lights all bloody night?

Tomas Where have you been? I didn't know—

Anna You've run the power right down! You braindead little worm!

> *ANNA flashes the torch in his face.*
>
> *He shields his eyes, afraid of her violent mood.*

Find some other hole to crawl into, worm. Get out!

Tomas I'm not going.

Anna I'm stuck here—missed my chance to get out—thanks to you hanging round like a bad smell. Whining at me. Stealing my food.

Tomas I never stole your food.

Anna [*as TOMAS*] 'Oh, where's my family? I'll cry and cry if I don't find my family.'

Tomas What? Why are you saying that?

Anna If I'm stuck in this shit hole, I want it to myself. Get out.

> *TOMAS doesn't move.*
>
> *ANNA shines the torch in his eyes.*
>
> *TOMAS hunches up, shielding his eyes from the torch beam.*

I don't want you here! Okay? So get your stinking carcass out of here!

Tomas You can't make me go.

> *ANNA stands over him, maybe threatening him with a hunk of rubble.*
>
> *Then she drops the rubble and lets the torch drop.*
>
> *TOMAS picks up the torch and uses it to see her more clearly.*

What happened? Where have you been all night?

Anna Don't ask me so many—Just shut up.

Tomas Are you hurt? Is that blood? What happened?

Anna Don't say anything.

> *He lets ANNA take back the torch.*
>
> *She turns it off and hunches up on her bed.*

Tomas Do you want me to turn off the lights?

> *ANNA doesn't respond.*

I mean, you don't have to do a story if you don't—

Anna Forget those stories. Airy-fairy bullshit. So sugary sweet they make my teeth ache.

Tomas They're not all sugary sweet.

Anna Childish crap. The stories in that stupid book—They trick people into thinking things work out all nice and fair in the end.

Tomas Well, some of them aren't—

Anna That's what you think, isn't it?

Tomas No. No, I think—

Anna Yeah, dopey farm boy thinks that all he has to do is—

Tomas No! You're not listening to me. I'm not some stupid little kid who believes every story like it's a real thing.

Anna Blah blah blah.

Tomas Listen to me! Don't just—Why are you—?

Anna Should I tell you the lovely story of what happened to me tonight? How people are scum—animals. But you couldn't handle it because—smart people can see it's all a hopeless mess out there and that's—

Tomas It's not all hopeless.

Anna Putting up your pathetic notes. 'Dear Mum and Dad, meet me at the railway station and we can skip off into the sunset.' It's not going to happen! You're kidding yourself!

Tomas You don't know everything!

Anna Do you really think your family is gonna turn up and it's going to be a happy ending? Wake up, moron!

Tomas You're a bitch and I'm not—

Anna A moron kidding himself.

Tomas Yeah? Shows how much you know. [*Brandishing the note*] I got a message about my brother. Saying he's okay. I'll find my brother soon. So you're the moron. Not me. You're the moron bitch.

Anna Hunh. Well, that's great for you.

> ANNA's angry energy suddenly vanishes.
> TOMAS instantly feels terrible.
> ANNA shrinks back into her bed.

Tomas Sorry.

Anna Don't say that.

Tomas No, but I mean I'm sorry for saying—I mean, I'm sorry if—

Anna Don't apologise because something good happened to you. Anyway, one note doesn't prove anything. I'm still right. The world is not like those stories.

Tomas I know that.

> *There's a silence as the two of them listen to the shelling around them.*

But the world isn't only like *this*. That's what I think, anyway.

> *TOMAS waits for ANNA to argue back. She doesn't say anything.*

What I like about the stories—it's not because everything turns out magically right—it's not like that. Sometimes the stories are like my grandparents talking to me even though they're dead. It's like secret treasures... Oh... If I try to think it in words it falls apart in my brain but I still know I like the—

Anna It's your brain that's falling apart.

Tomas I'll shut up then.

> *Silence.*
>
> *We hear ANNA sniff back tears.*

Anna? Are you okay? What happened?

> *She won't answer.*

Anna Hey—do one of the tales now.

Tomas Two seconds ago, you said the stories were crap.

Anna Better than listening to you fart and dribble over there. I don't want to sleep tonight. So talk.

Tomas Oh... I don't know if—

Anna Either you tell a story or I'll go for a walk outside until the sun comes up and leave you here on your own.

Tomas Don't do that.

Anna Well, talk.

Tomas Umm... okay... I don't know if I can do this properly.

> *ANNA growls at him.*

'The Ice Dragon and the She-Wolf'. Okay... umm... Many years ago—hundreds at least—in a faraway land, there was a valley of lush green fields. To the north lay snow-covered mountains ruled over by an Ice Dragon. When he felt like it, the dragon blew freezing winds down from the mountains just to annoy people.

In a pool of light we see VILLAGERS run through, rugged up, shivering.

The dragon was bigger than twelve elephants, covered in scales of ice as hard as iron, with claws that could slice a person in half with one swipe. It would slice people in half for no reason.

We hear the DRAGON's roaring and shrieking noises and maybe see its shadow overhead.

VILLAGERS dodge to avoid being sliced by the DRAGON.

The creature could fly at mighty speeds, using its huge wings. It dropped its enormous poos on the surrounding farms.

VILLAGERS watch dragon poo fall from the sky and then shovel it into wheelbarrows, faces scrunched up against the smell.

And you should know that dragon poo contains foul-smelling acid which burns the crops and ruins the land.

Anna Did you get all this from the book?

Tomas Well, I remembered other stuff and I smooshed bits together. If you want, I can—

Anna No. Keep going.

VILLAGERS run off with the wheelbarrows of poo.

Tomas So—umm, oh yeah… One day the dragon was flapping his wings to blow freezing winds across the land. A young man called Ivan wanted to escape the cold wind.

Ivan I'll shelter in this barn for the night.

IVAN huddles up inside a barn.

Tomas He was nodding off to sleep, when he saw a creature creep inside.

A WOLF comes into the barn and IVAN gasps in terror.

Ivan A she-wolf… I don't want to be dinner for a wolf!

IVAN begins to creep out without the WOLF seeing.

43

Tomas But then Ivan saw the most amazing sight. The she-wolf slipped off its skin and out stepped a lovely young woman.
Ivan Wow!

This startles the young woman, KATERINA.

Katerina Oh!
Ivan Don't be afraid. I won't hurt you.

IVAN calms KATERINA and they sit together.

Tomas The young woman explained that her name was—
Katerina Katerina.
Tomas She had been cursed by the Ice Dragon.
Ivan Why?
Katerina Because I refused to marry him. Now I can only shed my wolf skin under cover of darkness and when no one can see me.
Anna Well, Ivan saw her, so now what—
Tomas Wait. Ivan and Katerina talked and laughed together through the night.
Ivan Is there nothing I can do to break this curse?
Katerina Well, I'm told that if there's a man who truly loves me—
Ivan And here I am! Lucky.
Katerina If that man buries the wolf skin and never tells me where it is buried, I can remain a human being.
Ivan No worries. I'll bury this wretched wolf skin in a secret place.
Tomas So when the sun came up—
Katerina I'm free of the wolf curse at last!

IVAN and KATERINA embrace.

Tomas They married and soon had a baby daughter, Anoushka. Anoushka grew up to be a kind and clever girl.

ANOUSHKA runs on stage and flies into the arms of her parents who swing her around with joy.

Anna But then something crappy happens.
Tomas Well, yeah. The Ice Dragon was jealous and wanted Anoushka for himself. He scooped her up and stole her away to his icy kingdom.

ANOUSHKA is whisked away.

We hear the sound of the DRAGON shrieking or roaring.
IVAN and KATERINA try to hold onto her but she is swept out of their reach.

Ivan and Katerina wept for many days.

IVAN and KATERINA cling together in grief.

Katerina I'm afraid my heart will break into a thousand pieces.
Ivan There is no way we can travel there to save Anoushka.
Katerina There is one way. Fetch me my wolf skin.
Ivan What? No!
Katerina You must dig it up from the hiding place and bring it to me.
Ivan No, my darling Katerina. If you do this, you must remain a wolf forever!
Katerina Please. This is the only way to save our daughter.
Tomas Ivan begged and begged, but in the end—
Ivan I can see that your love for our daughter is stronger than anything in the universe.
Tomas Sadly, Ivan fetched the wolf skin.

IVAN gives KATERINA the wolf skin and she exits.

That night, Ivan watched a she-wolf run off from his house into the woods. He knew it was his beloved Katerina.

IVAN exits, heartbroken, as we follow the SHE-WOLF on her journey.
TOMAS picks up the torch and runs the torch beam along the jagged edges of the building, as if tracing the SHE-WOLF's journey.

The she-wolf ran for many days and nights across the vast desert of ice and across the jagged mountains beyond that. No human being could ever make this journey, and even the she-wolf was almost dead from exhaustion, her paws ragged and bleeding.

The SHE-WOLF stops for a moment, panting, licking her paws.

Eventually she reached the dragon's ice palace, with towers that went higher than anyone could see.

The SHE-WOLF prowls around the base of the castle and looks up at the towers.

The she-wolf prowled around the castle night after night, calling to her daughter.

Katerina Daughter! Anoushka! Come to the window!

Tomas Then one night—

Katerina Anoushka!

Tomas Anoushka appeared in a window of ice high up in the tower.

We see ANOUSHKA in the window, staring out.

Katerina Anoushka! It's me, your mother! I've come to rescue you!

Tomas But Anoushka didn't recognise her mother's voice. All Anoushka could hear was the howling of a she-wolf across the icy wastes.

Anoushka Nothing to see but ice and snow. Oh, I long to hear my mother's voice. I'm afraid I'll never see my dear mother again!

Tomas Then the she-wolf—

Anna Stop. No more of that story.

Tomas What? I was just getting to—

Anna I don't want to hear any more of that one.

Meanwhile ANOUSHKA is stuck in the tower and the SHE-WOLF prowls around below.

Tomas But it's okay in the end. It's really fantastic. This whole pack of she-wolves turns up and together they attack the dragon.

We hear the howling of other wolves who run on stage in a pack to join the SHE-WOLF.

The wolves get revenge for all the people the dragon killed and all the terrible things he did.

We hear the DRAGON's death throes.

They cut the dragon's heart into a thousand bloody pieces.

The SHE-WOLF, exhausted, wipes blood off her paws.

Anna I said I don't want to hear—

Tomas No no, but you have to hear because it's happy in the end. In the end, the she-wolf carries the girl home on her back and the curse gets broken and they all—

Anna I believe you. I just don't want to hear it.

ANNA watches KATERINA throw off her wolf skin.

46

She and ANOUSHKA reunite and go off together, arms entwined.

ANNA turns away as the lights fade on the story.

Tomas I thought that was a good story. Sorry if I told it badly.

Anna You didn't tell it badly.

Tomas Sorry if I upset you. I just—

Anna It's not your fault. You should know, carrot-boy, today I saw my mother running down the street.

Tomas Your mother? She's okay? Your mum's okay! Far out… Did you talk to her? Did she—?

Anna It's not that kind of story. It was Mum's coat. But not her.

Tomas What—you mean—?

Anna I used to be ninety-nine percent sure she was killed in the market. Now I'm a hundred percent sure.

Tomas Oh. Oh, Anna… I'm so sorry. I don't know what—

ANNA is fierce rather than grief-stricken at this moment.

Anna I've decided: when I get across the border, I'm never coming back. I hate this place.

Tomas I don't want to leave.

Anna It's different for you. You've still got family here.

Tomas Well, maybe I do.

Anna I'm going to have a great life in a place where lights come on when you flick the switch and where people don't put on black ski masks and shoot their neighbours. I'm lucky I've got no family to keep me in this country. What time is it?

Tomas Three or four, I think.

Anna I want to stay awake until it's light. Keep talking.

Tomas I can't think of any more stories. Sorry.

Anna I don't want to sleep tonight.

Tomas I guess I could remember one of the old ones—

Anna I've got one. It's about a hunter and a cooking pot.

Tomas I don't know this one.

Anna One day a hunter set out for the woods.

A HUNTER appears in a pool of light.

He bid farewell to his beloved wife and little son.

*The HUNTER'S WIFE appears holding their three-year-old SON
on her hip.*

*She waves goodbye and holds the little boy's hand to wave
goodbye too.*

*The HUNTER scoops up his SON and swings him around,
laughing. Then he hands his SON back to his WIFE.*

Hunter You go and play until I bring home deer meat to cook for
our dinner.

The HUNTER steps through the woods, searching for deer.

Anna He didn't realise that his son had followed him into the
woods, eager to help.

Hunter Ah!

Anna The hunter spotted some deer at the bottom of a steep gorge
and climbed down. When the little boy tried to follow his father
down, he slipped and fell into the gorge. The hunter recognised
that cry of terror in an instant.

Offstage, a child cries out.

Hunter My son!

Anna He ran back but there was nothing he could do. The hard and
unforgiving rocks had killed his son.

The HUNTER cradles the body of his dead SON.

The hunter thought his heart would surely break.

Hunter How can I tell his mother that her only child is dead?

Anna The hunter thought long and hard until he came up with a plan.

The HUNTER wraps the SON in a blanket and carries him off.

He carried the boy home in the blanket he usually used to wrap
the hunted deer. From outside the house, he called…

Hunter My darling! I'm back!

The HUNTER'S WIFE comes to the door.

Hunter's Wife And you've brought a fine deer! We will have a feast!

Hunter Yes, indeed. But we will have a special dish tonight. While
our son helps me chop the firewood, you must go and borrow a
cooking pot from one of our neighbours. For this special dish, we
need a pot that has never been used to cook a meal of sorrow.

The HUNTER carries the bundle off to one side.

Anna The hunter's wife went to the house of their neighbour.

The HUNTER'S WIFE knocks on the door and NEIGHBOUR 1 comes to the door.

Hunter's Wife We have deer meat for a wonderful feast. May I borrow your largest cooking pot?

Neighbour 1 Of course.

Maybe the NEIGHBOUR drags out a huge cooking pot.

Hunter's Wife I almost forgot—it must be a pot that has never been used to cook a meal of sorrow.

Neighbour 1 Oh, then I can't help you. This one was used to cook the meal after my husband died.

Anna The hunter's wife went to the next house with the same request.

NEIGHBOUR 2 drags out another huge cooking pot.

Hunter's Wife Thank you. That's a fine big pot. We need a pot that has never been used to cook a meal of sorrow.

Neighbour 2 I'm sorry to say we last used this pot on the day of our daughter's funeral.

Anna The hunter's wife knocked on every door in the village but could not find the pot she needed.

The HUNTER'S WIFE arrives home where the HUNTER waits with the bundle in his lap.

Hunter's Wife We may not be able to cook that special dish. No one could lend us a pot that has not been used to cook a meal of sorrow.

Hunter I suppose every house has tasted sorrow. And today it is our turn.

The HUNTER folds back the blanket to reveal their dead SON. The HUNTER'S WIFE throws herself down beside the body of the boy, weeping.
The HUNTER enfolds her and weeps too.

Anna The end.

Tomas The end? Oh… I didn't think it was gonna be that kind of story. When you said the hunter had a plan and there was the stuff about cooking the special dish, I thought he had some magic way to bring the kid back to life or… I didn't think—I mean, that ending snuck up on me and—

Anna It's only a made-up story in a book. We can change the ending if you like.

Suddenly hopeful, the HUNTER and his WIFE stand, lifting the child in their arms and look to ANNA.

Tomas How?

Anna Well, maybe the hunter could know about a magical way to use the pot to—

Tomas No. That's not right… It's not how that story is supposed to go.

Anna No.

Dejected, the HUNTER and his WIFE resume their original end position, weeping over the boy's body.

We could add a bit to the end.

Tomas Like what?

Anna That night, all the neighbours came to the hunter's house, bringing pots of food they'd cooked. They shared a meal and shared stories of their sorrows.

The NEIGHBOURS enter, carrying pots of food.

They sit with the HUNTER and his WIFE—eating, talking, embracing.

TOMAS watches the story scene for a while.

Tomas That's a better ending.

Anna Yes.

TOMAS can hear the tears in ANNA's voice. He's not sure what to say.

Tomas Was your mum a good cook?

Anna She was a fantastic cook. Especially cakes. She was a good teacher, y'know. Kids from her classes used to run up to her in the street. When I was little, I'd get jealous sometimes. She'd always joke with kids. She could find a way to joke about anything.

Tomas She sounds great, your mum.

ANNA nods, crying.
TOMAS peeks out the window.

It's getting light now.

Anna Good. Let's get out and go for a walk.

TOMAS and ANNA grab their usual scavenging bags and head out.

I'll walk up as far as the railway station with you. You can check if there's a message from your brother.

They exit.
Dawn light oozes into the house as the story characters fade.

Scene Six

Daytime. The railway station.
TOMAS has fallen asleep, hunched up near the message wall. He jerks awake.

Tomas How long have I been asleep?

Station Guard Maybe two hours. It'll be dark soon.

Tomas Oh no… Did anyone come past or— ?

Station Guard No one new has shown up today.

TOMAS gets to his feet, checks the clock, disappointed.

I think someone didn't get much sleep last night.

TOMAS shrugs and nods.

Tomas Well, guess I'll see you tomorrow.

Station Guard Same time, same place.

TOMAS heads off.
Just as he is about to exit, a seventeen-year-old boy, NICK, enters, not sure he's in the right place.

Hey! You.

The STATION GUARD reaches out to tap NICK on the shoulder.
NICK spins around fiercely, grabs the GUARD's arm, assuming he's being attacked.

51

The GUARD steps back, placating.

Take it easy, young man. Not everyone is out to hurt you.

The GUARD points out TOMAS.

Nick Tomas?

TOMAS turns and sees NICK.
He runs back and they embrace, laughing, breathless.

Tomas [*to the STATION GUARD*] This is Nick. This is my brother. He's alive. He's okay.
Station Guard [*laughing*] I can see that.
Tomas [*to NICK*] What about everyone else? Are they—?
Nick Mum, the girls, Grandma—they're all safe.
Tomas And Dad?
Nick We're not sure. But I'm looking. We'll find him.
Tomas So is everyone back home?
Nick Mum and the girls are in a camp, in a safe part. Tomorrow morning, as soon as the curfew lifts, we'll go. I know a guy with a van.

TOMAS is laughing, confused, his head spinning.

Tomas A van, right. In the morning. Okay.

NICK suddenly stumbles, his injured leg giving way.
TOMAS grabs his brother to steady him.

Whoa… you okay? Is your leg bad?
Nick I just need to rest.
Tomas I know somewhere we can stay tonight.
Nick Somewhere safe? It needs to be somewhere—
Tomas Yeah, yeah. It's a good place.

TOMAS leads NICK off.
At the last moment, he turns and waves goodbye to the STATION GUARD.

Station Guard Good luck.

Scene Seven

Night. The house.

NICK and TOMAS enter. NICK is exhausted, wincing with the pain of his leg injury. TOMAS is babbling happily.

Tomas Anna should be back any minute. She usually manages to get back before the curfew. Check this out.

> *TOMAS turns on the party lights attached to a battery.*

Anna set this up. We had to get a new battery this morning. Cost a few American dollars but worth it, I reckon.

Nick American dollars? Have you got more?

Tomas It's Anna's money. You'll like Anna—well, maybe you won't. She can be testy to start off. But once you get to know her, she's cool and—

> *TOMAS sees a note attached with chewing gum near ANNA's bed.*

Nick [*reading the front of the note*] 'Carrot-boy'. Eh?

Tomas That's me.

> *TOMAS takes down the note and reads it.*

Oh… Anna's gone. She's going across the border, west.

Nick Across the—? How's she going to do that?

Tomas She must have a plan.

Nick Your friend's crazy. How's she gonna get that far? Even if she makes it to the border, they'll hand her straight over to the soldiers.

Tomas Well, I don't know. I guess… [*Reading the note*] 'PS: I took the book. I can sell it for real dollars. Sorry.' Ha. Fair enough.

> *NICK isn't listening—he's taking off his boots, exhausted, in pain.*

Nick Listen, I've been travelling for three days straight. I really need to sleep.

Tomas Oh, sure. You can have Anna's bed.

> *TOMAS hurries to unroll ANNA's bed for his brother.*

53

Nick That's good. Ta.

TOMAS sets up his own bed.

NICK lies down, ready to flake.

TOMAS lies down too but he's wide awake and jittery.

Tomas I don't think I can sleep. My head's buzzing with too much stuff.

Nick Ohhh, Tomas, come on… We have to get up early to get to the van.

Tomas Sorry.

TOMAS tries to shut up. He lasts two seconds.

I wonder what's happening to Anna right now. I hope she's okay.

Nick Mate, I don't want to get you worried about your friend but honestly, it's likely—

Tomas Have you seen what it's like at the border? Do you reckon if Anna—?

Nick I don't know. I can't think one more thought or work out one more plan or hope about one more thing. I just need to sleep.

NICK curls up to sleep again.

Tomas She's smart as anything. She'll work stuff out.

Nick Tomas, I don't—look, I hope you're right.

Tomas Anna, she'd travel at night and hide out in the day. She'd be okay for food because she'll swap the book for a tin of condensed milk.

In a pool of light ANNA appears, tipping condensed milk into her mouth.

Only it'd be genuine magical-type condensed milk that refills itself when it's empty.

Nick Eh?

NICK is awake now, following the story along with TOMAS.

Tomas And she meets a farm boy—an incredibly clever, hot-looking farmboy—and they travel together.

A BOY joins ANNA as she marches through the country.

54

Anna Do you realise you have a potato growing out of the back of your head?

Potato-head Boy Oh, yeah. An elf gave me three wishes and I kind of messed up.

Tomas So Anna and the potato-head boy feast on mashed potato with heaps of butter. Every day a new potato grows on his head so they never run out.

Nick What happens when they get to the border?

Tomas Uh… Well, the potato-head boy says goodbye.

Potato-head Boy I'm staying here. I've got to meet up with my family.

Anna Fair enough. See you round.

> *The POTATO-HEAD BOY goes.*

Tomas At the border, Anna transforms herself into a cat to slip through fences without any soldiers seeing. On the other side of the border, she transforms back into Anna.

> *TOMAS hesitates as ANNA almost walks out of view.*

Nick Is that it?

Tomas No. Wait. She stops to rest by a river and floating towards her comes an oakwood chest with shiny brass hinges.

> *ANNA hoists a wooden chest out of the river.*

Inside are photos of her family and schoolfriends and her mum. Underneath the photos, she finds dozens of magnificent amber pendants. Trapped inside the amber there are dragonflies and beetles and dinosaurs.

Nick [*laughing*] Dinosaurs?

Tomas Very small ones. Anna keeps the pendant with the bee, the one that belonged to her mother.

> *ANNA puts that pendant around her neck.*

She sells the rest and gets a suitcase full of American dollars.

> *ANNA trades the amber for a suitcase bulging with cash.*

Once she gets to Paris—

Nick Paris. Very nice.

Tomas   —with the American dollars, Anna buys the most beautiful house in Paris. And then once a year—on her mother's birthday— she throws a party, even though her mother's dead.

Various characters enter. They bring in strings of party lights and other party paraphernalia.

Anyone in Paris who's having a crappy time and needs a party, they'd be invited. Everyone cooks Anna's mum's favourite recipes and cakes.

People bring on huge cooking pots and cakes.
Others bring on musical instruments made from bones.
They greet each other warmly.

And they eat and play music on instruments made from singing bones and tell jokes all night. The potato-head boy travels to Paris for the party too.

ANNA and the POTATO-HEAD BOY are reunited.

And—and then... uh...

TOMAS falls silent, unable to think of what to say next.
The music fades and story characters stop.
They all look to TOMAS, waiting for the next bit of the story.

I hope she's all right.

The lights fade to blackout.

THE END

www.ingramcontent.com/pod-product-compliance
Lightning Source LLC
Chambersburg PA
CBHW041933090426
42744CB00017B/2041